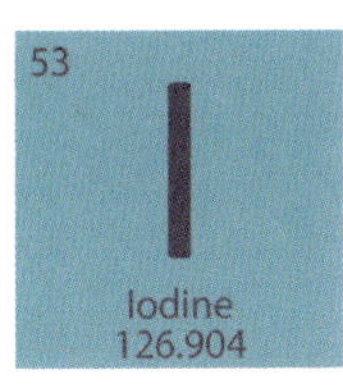

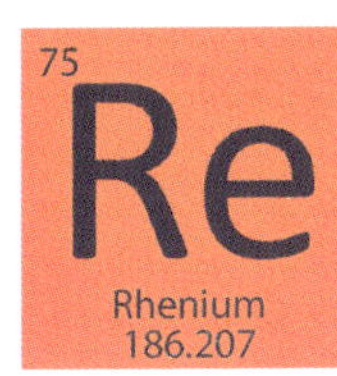

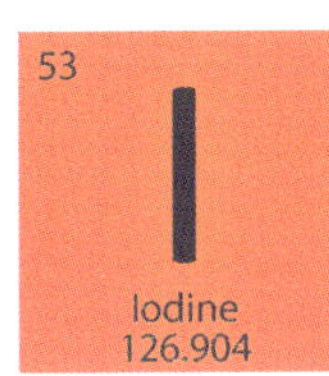

Feeding inquisitive minds

Dedicated to my friends and family. Thank you for your love and support.

SciRecipes Cookbook of Curiosity by Joanna Morris

Published by Totally Roarsome Books

First published in Great Britain 2019

First edition

ISBN 978-1-5272-5104-5

Written and Illustrated by Joanna Morris

Cover by Joanna Morris

Please send correspondence to

enquire@scirecipes.co.uk

SciRecipes
Unit 5, Cobden Chamber, Pelham Street
Floor 2, Cobden Place
Nottingham
NG1 2ED

To learn more about SciRecipes please go to www.scirecipes.co.uk

Our mission

I often meet people who, when they find out I'm a geologist, have a lot of questions about the science of the earth. It has made me realise that whilst curiosity can exist into adulthood there are barriers to continued learning. The reasons for this are varied; from a lack of confidence, expense, or poor access to places to search for answers. This cookbook is an alternative way to learn science. It should appeal to those that enjoy food, don't like waste and are not afraid to express their creative flair.

Science and Engineering are changing and our future depends on the diversity of ideas created by many minds. Here at SciRecipes we believe everyone should have an opportunity to learn and express themselves in a way that suits them. So, throw out the traditional textbooks and give this a go instead.

How does SciRecipes work

SciRecipes smashes together science and baking to turn the complex into something simple and tasty. Whether you are perplexed by pulsars or flummoxed by fusion our mission is to teach everyone a little more about the planet they live on and the scientific principles that govern it.

We do this by taking everyday recipes and twisting them with science. For example, Journey to the Centre of the Pizza uses different toppings to teach you the different layers of the Earth. The 'sciency bit' describes what the different layers are made of and some history behind the discovery. Each SciRecipe is split into two parts.

First the recipe that contains step-by-step illustrated guides.

Simply follow the instructions to make some delicious treats.

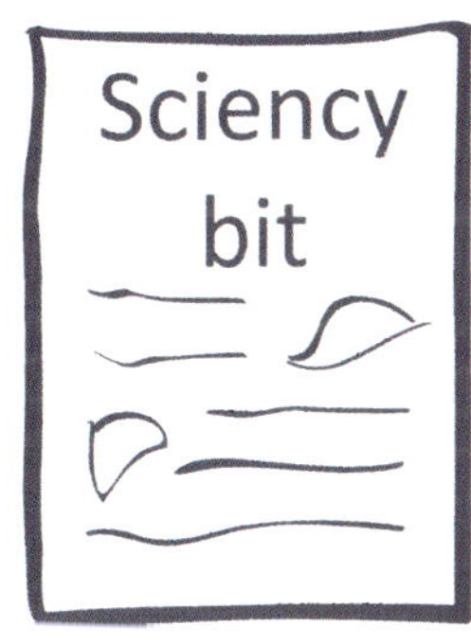

The second part is the 'sciency bit'.

Sit back, relax and learn what science your treats are all about

There is a mix of sweet and savoury recipes covering a wide range of topics from Earth, to Life, to Space. If you're not sure where to start turn to page 5 to choose your own SciRecipes adventure!

About the author

Jo Morris is an award-winning science communicator and food producer. She spent eight years studying geosciences at university that provided opportunities to travel the world in search of volcanoes and fossils. In 2015 she travelled to Madagascar to study the flora and fauna of mangroves. In her spare time, she likes to grow vegetables, try out tasty recipes, train for triathlons and spend time with family and friends.

To share her scientific passion, she set up SciRecipes in 2016. She is now learning how to run her own business, writing updates on her Geology Girl Rocks blog and will soon be creating a charity called The GGR Foundation. She has learnt some really cool stuff and her aim is to share it with you.

Contents

Pick you own SciRecipes adventure

If you are unsure about what you want to learn or bake first then here is the answer! Start at the beginning by choosing your favourite hobby and continue on step-by-step with each question. Choose a different adventure each time to keep learning new things.

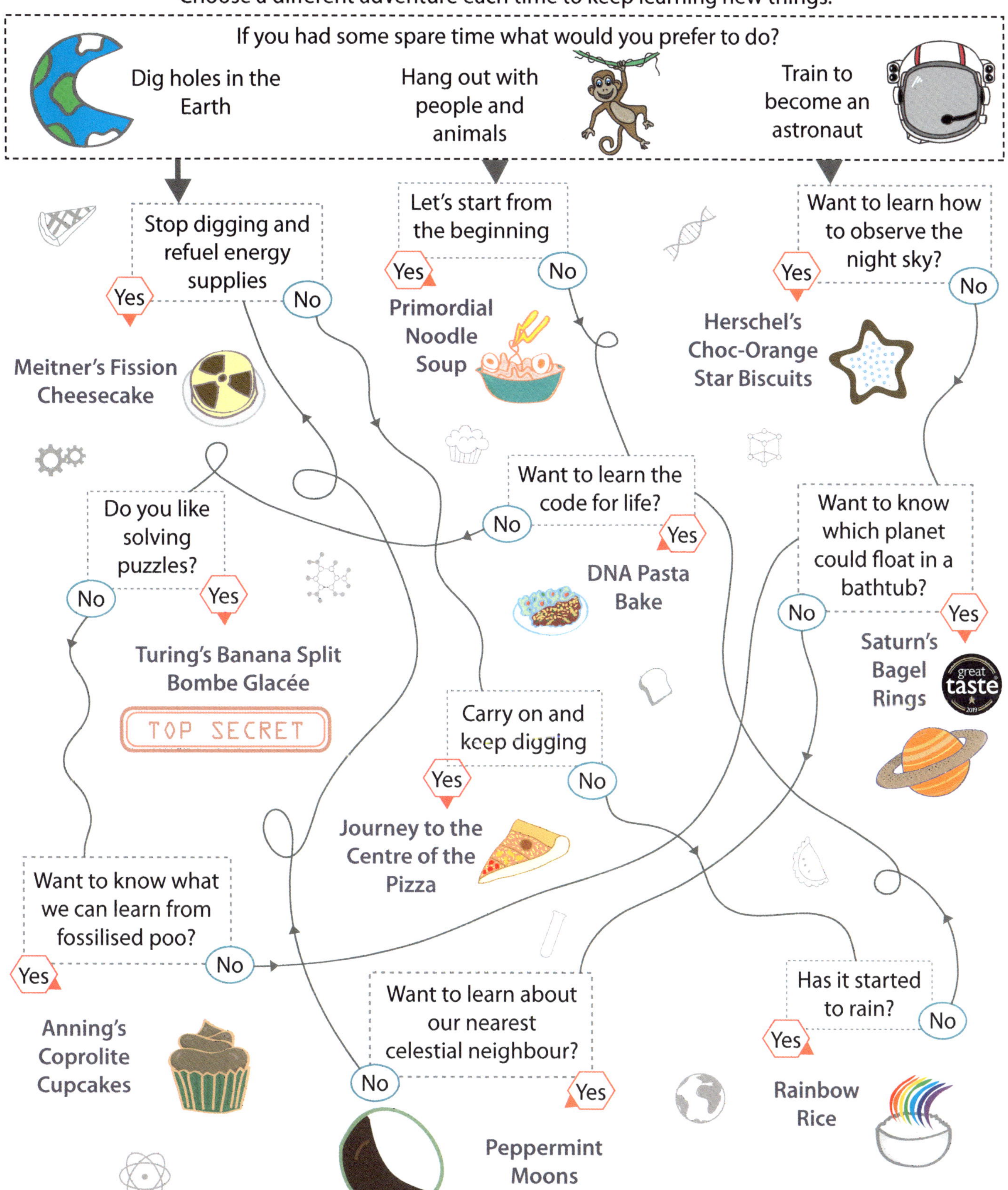

Bake with Jake Top Tips

Hi there! I'm Jake and I've got loads of top tips to help you bake. You will see me throughout this recipe book with helpful information that will make you a rock star in the kitchen.

If you bake or cook regularly then dive right in. If not, then the next three pages will help you navigate your way through the kitchen

Recipe Guide

Every recipe has a guide to show you how easy or difficult it might be. Some may take a few minutes or only have a few ingredients. Others require more time, have more ingredients or more complex steps to follow.

STUDENT BAKER
quick and simple

MASTER CHEF
may take longer

CHEF PhD
tricky but yummy

Measurements

g - gram
kg - kilogram
ml - millilitres
tsp - tea spoon
tbsp - table spoon

Oven temperature

°C - degrees Celsius

Temperatures for SciRecipes are for a fan assisted oven.

Times may need to adjusted if you bake in something different.

Cleaning up

Our top tip is to run a bowl of hot soapy water before you begin. Have a cloth ready and clean up as you go. Most of the recipes need some cooking time in the oven. This is the best opportunity to wash-up, load the dishwasher and tidy. Put some music on, sing loudly and it will be done in no time!

Baking terms

These are some phrases you may see throughout the book with their definitions.

'beat the egg'
This means that you need to mix the egg white and yolk together before using it. Break the egg into a bowl and use a fork or a whisk to mix it.

'cream butter and sugar'
This simple step will make your cake taste delicious. It allows for the sugar to dissolve into the water and adds air bubbles in the batter which will expand when baked.

'dice vegetables'
Take a sharp knife and cut pieces into squares that measure one centimetre on each side.

'knead'
This is an important process when baking bread. When kneading by hand, hold the dough with the fingers of one hand. Using the palm of the other push the dough away from you to stretch it out. Take the end furthest way from you and fold it back on top of the dough. Turn it round by 90 degrees and repeat the process. The dough will be stretchy and smooth when you are done.

'knock back'
This is a term required when baking with bread dough. After proving a dough, the air needs 'knocking' out. Make a fist with your hand and gently punch the dough slowly.

'roll out'
This is for when you need to make a ball of dough into something flat. A rolling pin is the best thing to use but if you don't have one then something like a wine bottle will do the trick. Roll slowly and press with even pressure. This way the dough stays the same thickness throughout.

'sift'
In the past this was done to remove any impurities from the bags of flour, such as brick dust. Today that isn't as important but it will stop you getting lumps in your batter. Hold the sieve in one hand and gentle bang the side with the palm of the other.

'zest'
This requires grating the skin of a citrus fruit such as lemon. Either use a micro planer or the smallest holes on a cheese grater. Be careful not to grate too deep as the white pith is bitter and won't make your food taste nice.

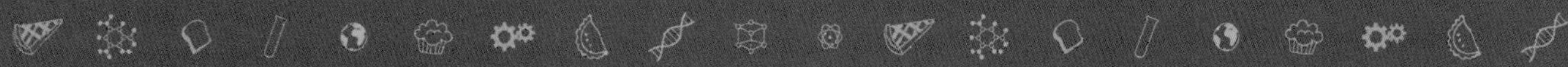

Alternative ingredients

Each ScRecipe has been designed to teach a scientific principle. Careful thought is put into the design and choice of ingredients in order to make each one as memorable as possible. In some cases this means choosing ingredients that some people choose not to eat or are allergic to. This doesn't mean that you can't make a SciRecipe, substitutions can be easily made for most of them.

Vegetarians
Most of the recipes in this book are suitable for vegetarians. For Journey to the Centre of the Pizza use slices of tomato instead of pepperoni, use vegetarian sausages for Rainbow Rice, use tofu in Primordial Noodle Soup and vegetarian chicken in Franklin's DNA Pasta Bake.

Vegan

All but one recipe, Saturn's Bagel Rings, contain ingredients not suitable for a vegan diet. There isn't enough room to list substitutions for each recipe here. We recommend to follow the instructions for the construction of a SciRecipe whilst following an alternative vegan recipe.

Gluten free (GF)

Most recipes can be swapped for GF flour. The exceptions will be the ones that feature bread dough. For Saturn Bagel Rings we recommend making GF doughnut rings and for Journey to the Centre of the Pizza we recommend buying GF pizza bases.

Top tips

Here are some top tips to help you perfect your SciRecipes.

Measuring water

If you don't have a measuring jug you can weigh your water instead. 100 ml of water weighs 100 grams.

Filling a piping bag

Step 1
Put the pointy end of the bag into a tall glass. Roll the top of the bag around the outside edge of the glass

Step 2
Fill the bag with mixture

Step 3
Collect the top of the bag together and seal with elastic band

Step 4
When you are ready to decorate cut the pointy end to form a nozzle.

Breaking an egg

Step 1
If you don't feel confident about breaking eggs straight into a mixture try breaking them into another bowl first.

Step 2
If you accidently get some shell fragments in your bowl, wet your finger first before picking it out.

Cooking time

Step 1
This will vary depending on your skill and confidence in the kitchen. Make sure you give yourself enough time to prepare the ingredients as well as the cooking time.

Step 2
Some recipes can be prepared in advance and is stated throughout the cookbook. More attention needs to be paid to the baking time of sweet dishes as they can easily burn if left in for too long.

Cooking meat

Step 1
Take out of fridge to room temperature. Season with salt and pepper. Always wash hands and surfaces. Don't use the same utensils from raw to cooked meat.

Step 2
Cook until juices run clear. If unsure take a knife and cut through meat. Do this if BBQing as temperatures can vary throughout cooking time.

SPACE

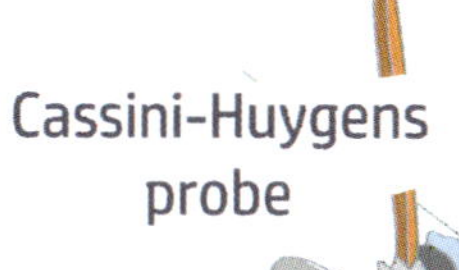

Cassini-Huygens probe

This recipe is designed to teach you about how we use telescopes to look at stars. You will learn about the different types of optical telescopes that can be used, Caroline Herschel who was one of the first people to make observations with them and the best place to build them.

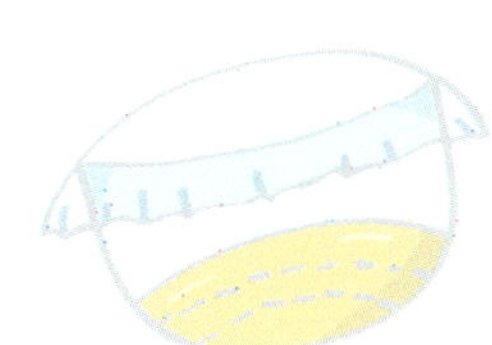

Caroline Herschel

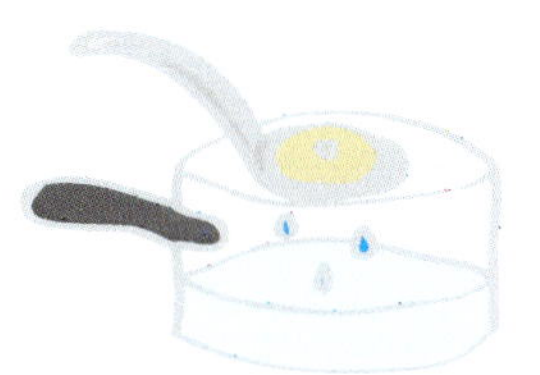

Hubble Space Telescope

These bagels will fill your house with the most amazing baked bread smell. Have a go at making a Great Taste 2019 award winning recipe to learn all about the sixth planet from our sun, Saturn.

Learn about our rocky partner in the night sky with this really easy peppermint patty recipe. Find out how it was formed, how old it is and who was the first scientist to step foot on it.

Saturn V rocket

Herschel's Choc-Orange Star Biscuits

Stars are amazing but they are really far away and difficult to see. This recipe for glittery chocolate orange biscuits helps to explain how telescopes work, how they improved our understanding of the universe and the first woman to be awarded a gold medal from the Astronomical Society.

Jake the dino top tips

You will need
- cling film
- rolling pin
- greaseproof paper
- baking tray
- piping bag
- star shaped cutter

Biscuit Ingredients

185 g softened butter
250 g caster sugar
1 egg
Zest of one orange
185 g plain flour
90 g cocoa powder
1 1/4 tsp baking powder

Frosting Ingredients

150 g icing sugar
Juice of one orange

Decorating Ingredients

Edible glitter

Step 1
Cream the butter and sugar until pale and creamy

Step 2
Add egg and orange zest. Mix

Step 3
Sift in dry ingredients and stir to combine

Step 4
Wrap the dough in cling film and leave to chill in fridge for 30 minutes

Step 5
Pre-heat oven to 180°C

Step 6
Roll out dough on a floured work surface until ½ cm thick. Use star cutter to cut dough

Step 7
Place on baking tray lined with greaseproof paper

Step 8
Bake for 10–12 minutes

Step 9
Take out of the oven and carefully place on cooling rack

Step 10
Mix orange juice and sifted icing sugar into a thick paste

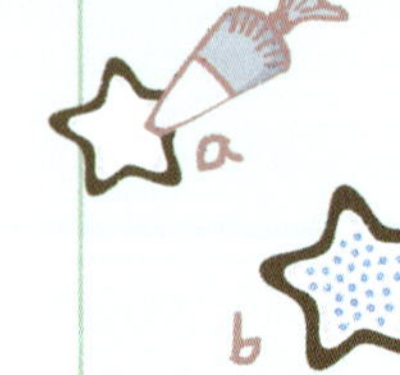

Step 11
Spoon into piping bag and cut a 5 mm nozzle

Step 12
Decorate with icing before sprinkling glitter over them

Storage
Keep in an air tight tin. Eat within five days

The Sciency Bit - Twinkle Twinkle Little Star

Our eyes are amazing tools for experiencing the world around us but when it comes to observing stars they need a little help. Astronomers build telescopes in order to see distant celestial objects. The earliest known record of a telescope is a 1608 patent submitted to the Netherlands government by Hans Lippershey.

How do telescopes work?

Telescopes can be built to detect different types of waves from across the electromagnetic spectrum. An optical telescope is designed to collect and focus visible light. This means that you can look at stars without the need of a computer to process an image. There are three main ways for an optical telescope to be made; reflecting, refracting and catadioptrical.

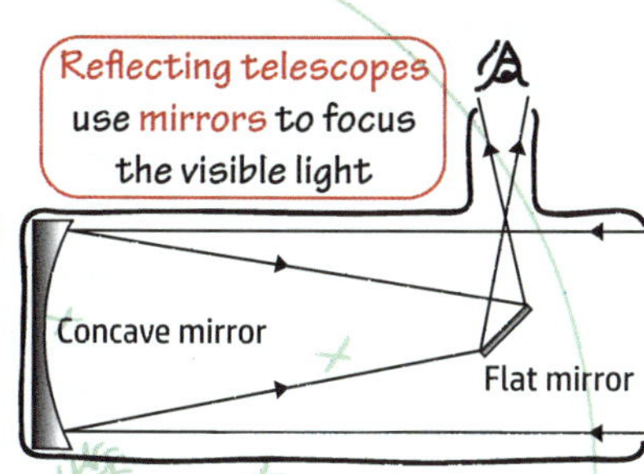

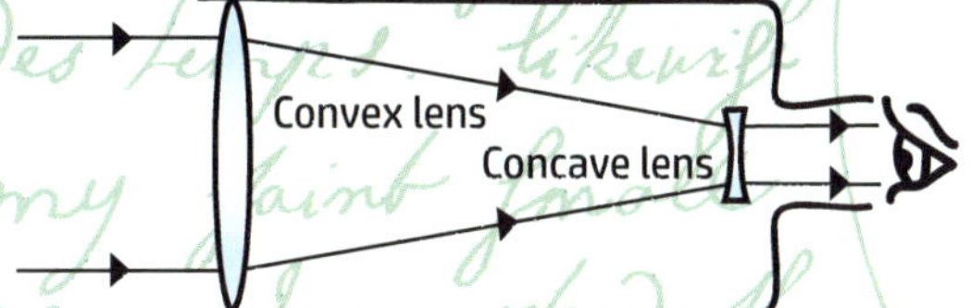

Refracting telescopes use lenses to focus the visible light

Catadioptrical telescopes
Use a combination of mirrors and lenses to produce and image in the eyepiece

Caroline Herschel was the first woman to be awarded a Gold Medal of the Royal Astronomical Society in 1828. As the younger sister of astronomer of William Herschel she was able to assist him with his observations. Together they spent many hours polishing mirrors in order to build some of the most powerful telescopes of the time. Over the many years of nightly observations she made many discoveries. On the 26th February 1783 she found two nebulae that had not been recorded before. After her brother had built her a comet-searching telescope she discovered eight comets throughout 1786-97. With her brother she made over 2400 discoveries of astronomical objects over 20 years and became the first woman to receive a salary for services to science.

Caroline Herschel

Where to build telescopes

The Earth's atmosphere can distort or block certain wavelengths on the electromagnetic spectrum. Telescopes have to be designed and built around the Earth in order to get the best possible image.

To see further and fainter objects each generation of telescope has gotten bigger. In 1789 the Herschel's designed a telescope with 1.2 meter diameter mirror. In 2022 the European Southern Observatory will open the world's largest optical telescope with a mirror that is 39.3 meters in diameter.

Hubble Space Telescope

Named after the astronomer Edwin Hubble, it was launched in 1990 on the Space Shuttle Atlantis. It orbits well above the Earth's atmosphere so it can take extremely high-resolution images without distortion.

Mauna Kea Observatories. Hawaii, USA

The best place to build an Earth based telescope is as high up as possible, somewhere with clean air, good weather and a low latitude location to reduce the amount of atmosphere that distorts visible light. The summit of Mauna Kea has a number of astronomical research facilities that take advantage of these perfect conditions.

Why not visit?

The National Space Centre is in Leicester, UK. It has a replica of Herschel's telescope as well as many other exhibits such as rockets, space suits, meteorites as well as the UK's largest planetarium.

Saturn's Bagel Rings

Makes 8

great taste 2019

Have a go at making this Great Taste 2019 award winning recipe to learn all about the planet Saturn. The chewy texture of bagels is achieved by boiling the dough before baking. Read the sciency bit to discover about the sixth planet in the solar system and how its famous rings formed.

Bagel Ingredients

- 500 g strong bread flour
- 7 g fast action yeast
- 1 ½ tbsp sugar
- 1 ½ tsp salt
- 250 ml warm water
- 1 tbsp bicarbonate of soda
- oil for greasing

Optional Ingredients

- 1 egg (beaten)
- poppy or sesame seeds

Jake the dino top tips

You will need

- cling film
- pan
- slotted spoon
- baking tray

Step 1

Mix flour, yeast, sugar and salt in a bowl before adding warm water

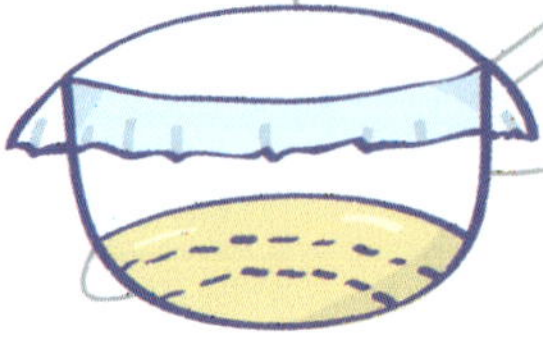

Step 2

Mix and knead for 10 minutes to smooth and elastic dough

Step 3

Put in oiled bowl, cover in cling film. Leave somewhere warm for 1 hour

Step 4

Knock air out and split into 8 pieces

Step 5

Shape into a ball. Use floured finger to make a hole and pull gently into a ring

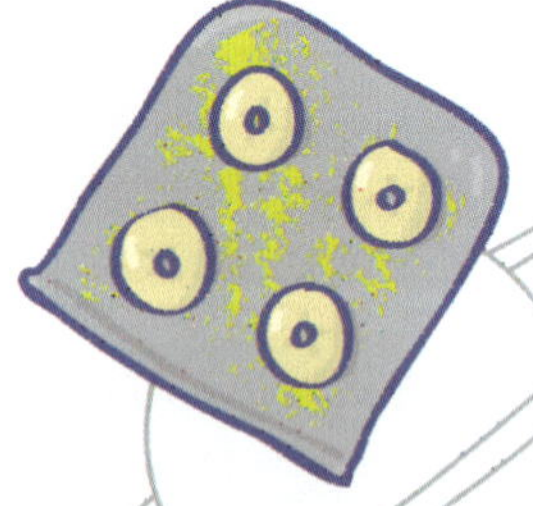

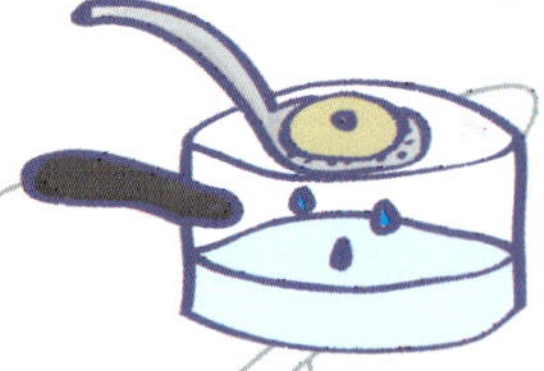

Step 6

Place on oiled baking tray and rest for 10 minute. Pre-heat oven to 220°C

Step 7

Fill a large pan with water and add bicarbonate of soda. Bring to a simmer

Step 8

Place 1-2 bagels in water and cook for 30 seconds on each side

Step 9

Use a slotted spoon to drain each bagel carefully

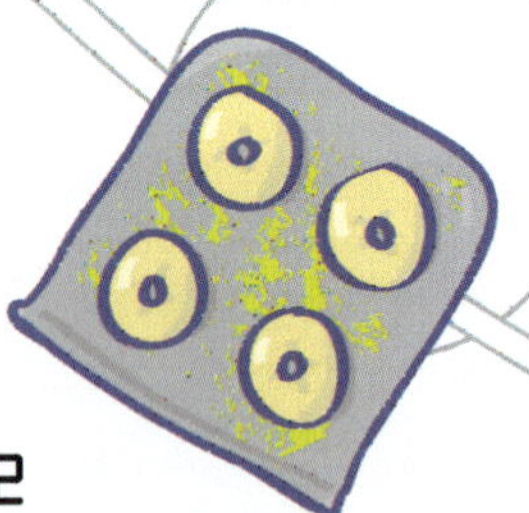

Step 10

Place back on oiled tray. Optional: glaze with beaten egg and sprinkle with seeds

Step 11

Turn the oven down to 190°C. Bake for 18 minutes until golden

Step 12

Leave on a wire rack to cool

Storage

Keep in an air tight tin. Eat within four days

THE SCIENCY BIT - "Put a ring on it!"

Saturn is the sixth planet from the sun and the second-largest in the Solar System. It is classed as a gas giant as it does not have a rocky surface. The length of a day on Saturn is 10 hours and 39 minutes. This is very fast and as a result the planet bulges at the equator. It takes 29 earth years for Saturn to orbit the sun.

Exploring Saturn

Saturn has been observed from Earth as early as prehistoric times and was included in many mythologies. It wasn't until telescopes were built and developed in the 17th century that detailed observations could be made.

Pioneer 11 was the first probe to flyby Saturn in 1979. In 2004 the Cassini-Huygens space probe entered Saturn's orbit. It spent 13 years observing the planet, rings and moons. On the 15th September 2017 it entered Saturn's atmosphere and was destroyed. It collected so much data throughout its mission that scientists are still making discoveries.

Cassini-Huygens probe

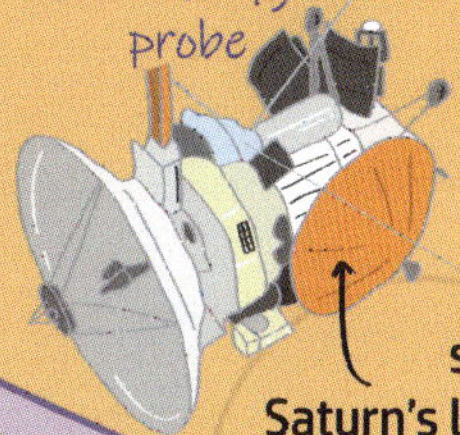

The Huygens probe detached from Cassini in order to descend to the surface of Saturn's largest moon, Titan.

Did you know?

Saturn has the lowest density of all the planets in the solar system.

Its density is less than water so if you had a bath tub big enough, Saturn would float.

Internal structure

Saturn is predominantly composed of hydrogen and helium. The closer to the core of Saturn the temperature, pressure and density increases. This means that the gasses turn into liquid and then solid the deeper down you go.

Rocky core

Ices

Metallic hydrogen & helium
responsible for Saturn's magnetic field

Helium rain

Liquid hydrogen
Helium is depleted in the outer layers of the planet as it forms droplets and falls towards the centre

Gassy hydrogen
Wind speeds can reach up to 1800 km/h

Rings of Saturn

The rings of Saturn are made of water, ice and small amounts of rocky material. The range in size from a micrometer (one thousandth of a millimeter) to a meter. The rings are 282,000 km wide and no more than 1 km thick.

Names of the rings

The rings can be grouped into major divisions based on their brightness and density.

- D ring
- C ring
- B ring
- Casini division
- A ring
- Roche division
- F ring
- G ring
- E ring

How did the rings form?

There is no consensus between scientists about how the formation of the rings. In 2019 data from the Cassini probe was published suggesting that the rings are no more than 100 million years old. This means the rings didn't form when the planet did 4.5 billion years ago. They are most likely formed from remnants of a moon that was destroyed from a collision with a comet.

Why not visit?

Visiting Saturn in person may not happen in our lifetime but it is possible to view Saturn through a decent telescope. Try and find a local astronomy club, pop along and ask to look at this amazing planet.

The Moons of Saturn

Saturn has 62 known moons, 53 of which have been formally identified and named. Most of Saturn's moons have been named after Titans of Greek mythology. They are exciting for planetary scientists to study as some have been identified as harbouring possible life. Future missions to Saturn will focus on these moons.

Titan

is Saturn's largest moon. It has a dense atmosphere and methane lakes on its surface. It is considered one of the best places to search for life in our Solar System. Space agencies around the world have a number of conceptual missions to further explore the surface. One includes landing a probe to float and explore the surface of the lakes.

Iapetus

is the third-largest moon. It is best known for its two-tone colouration and a 20 km high ridge running three quarters of the way around the equator.

Enceladus

orbits Saturn within the E ring and is mostly covered by fresh, clean ice. It has several exciting geological features including tectonics. The Cassini probe discovered cryovolcanoes near the south pole.

Mimas

is known for its giant impact crater, named Herschel, that measures 130 km across. The central peak rises 6 km above the crater floor. The moon is made up of mostly ice with only a small amount of rock.

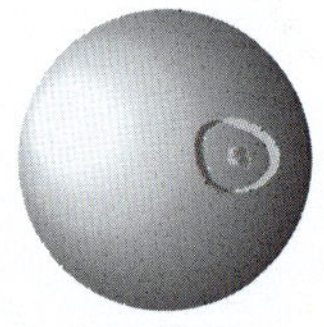

Peppermint Moons

Learn about our rocky partner in the night sky with this really easy peppermint patty recipe. Find out how it was formed, how old it is and who was the first to step foot on it.

Patty Ingredients

480 g icing sugar
240 g condensed milk
7 g powdered mint leaves
or peppermint essence

Decoration Ingredients

100 g dark chocolate

Makes 28

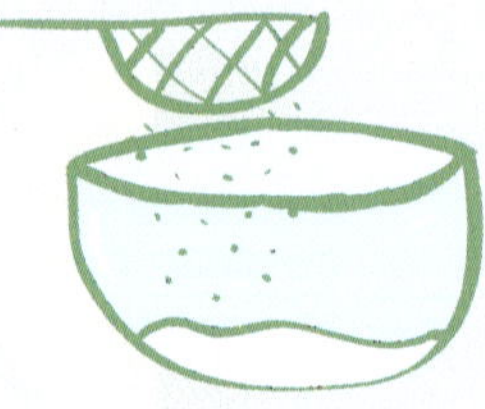

Step 1
Sift icing sugar and powdered mint leaves. If using essence use at next step

Step 2
Mix in condensed milk to form a dough

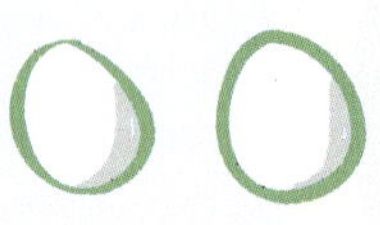

Step 3
Knead to a dough and split in half

Step 4
Roll each half into a sausage shape 14 cm long onto surface sprinkled with icing sugar

Step 5
Carefully cut each into 14 pieces and reshape into circles. Use spare icing sugar to coat hands to stop sticking

Step 6
Lay flat and leave for 2-3 hours to dry out

Step 7
Melt chocolate in a glass bowl over a simmering pan of water

Step 8
Dip the patties into the chocolate. Dip each one in slightly more chocolate to create different crescent shapes

Step 9
Display your patties in a circle to show the Moon's waxing and waning crescent cycle

Storage
Store in an airtight tin. Eat within five days

THE SCIENCY BIT

One small step for man...

The Moon is the Earth's only natural satellite. It is thought to have formed 4.51 billion years ago after a giant impact between Earth and a Mars-sized object called Theia. It orbits the Earth at an average distance of 384,400 km.

Moon Phases

It takes 28 days for the Moon to orbit the Earth. A day on the moon also lasts 28 days which is why the same side of the Moon is always facing us.

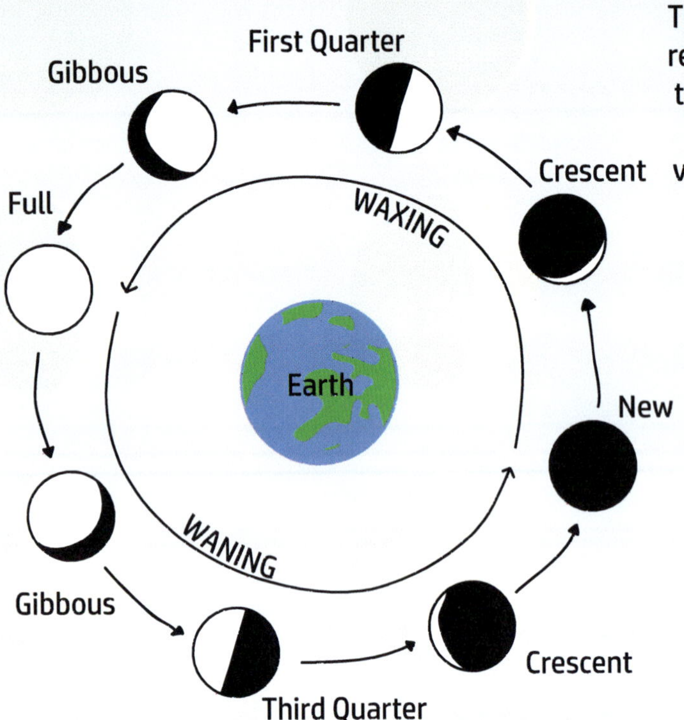

The Moon doesn't produce its own light so we rely on the Sun's light reflecting on the surface to see it. As it travels around the Earth certain portions of the lit side of the Moon become visible. It is this cyclical pattern that gives rise to the waxing and waning of crescent shapes.

Saturn V - The rocket built to send the astronauts to the moon. To date this is the most powerful rocket ever to be built and put into operation

Race to the Moon

The Great Space Race of the 1950s and 60s saw the Russians and Americans fight their way to be the first to conquer outer space. It was President John F. Kennedy's speech "of landing a man on the Moon and returning him safely to the Earth" that led the Americans to launch the Apollo Programme.

In 1969 Neil Armstrong became the first man to walk on the Moon. In total 12 men would walk on the surface and perform scientific experiments such as collecting moon rock samples, measuring solar wind and detecting 'moonquakes'.

Did you know?

The only scientist to walk on the moon was a geologist. His name was Harrison 'Jack' Schmitt and whilst the other astronauts were test pilots taught to do scientific experiments he was a scientist taught to fly the lunar module.

LIFE

Anning's Coprolite Cupcakes 18

The swirl of creamy, chocolate buttercream, atop a vanilla sponge cupcake, is piped to look like fossilised poo in this recipe. It may sound disgusting but finding a piece of coprolite can help us learn a lot about prehistoric animals

Ichthyosaur

Franklin's DNA Pasta Bake 20

Four of the main ingredients in this recipe start with the same letters that make up the four amino acids in DNA. Garlic, Chorizo, Tomato and Asparagus represents Guanine, Cytosine, Thyamine and Adenine respectively. This recipe can be prepared in advance and whilst it is cooking you learn more about the code that defines what you look like.

Rosalind Franklin

Primordial Noodle Soup 22

Known as the building blocks for life, DNA is the microscopic structure that defines how every living thing on Earth grows. The term 'primordial soup' is a name given to a theory about the very beginnings of how life got started on Earth.

Turing's Banana Split Bombe Glacée 24

The Bombe machine was designed by Alan Turing throughout World War II in order to break the Enigma code. A Bombe Glacée is a frozen dessert covered in melted chocolate and whipped cream. Decipher the code to work out the ingredients you need before you start.

Enigma machine

Anning's Coprolite Cupcakes

Makes 12

Cake ingredients

170 g salted butter
170 g caster sugar
1 tsp vanilla essence
3 eggs
170 g plain flour
1 ½ tsp baking powder

Frosting ingredients

400 g icing sugar
70 g cocoa powder
50 ml coffee
330 g salted butter

Jake the dino top tips

You will need
- Muffin tin
- 12 cupcake cases
- Cooling rack

Step 1
Pre-heat oven to 180 °C

Step 2
Beat butter and sugar together until pale and fluffy

Step 3
Add vanilla essence and mix

Step 4
Add one egg with 1 tbsp of sifted flour and mix

Step 5
Repeat step 4 twice with the other two eggs

Step 6
Mix in the rest of the sifted flour and baking powder

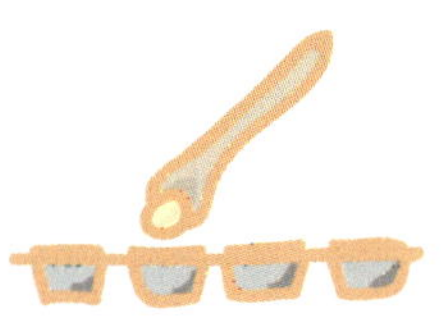

Step 7
Spoon 2 tbsp of mixture to each cupcake case

Step 8
Bake in the oven for 25 minutes. Do NOT open oven until the time is up

Step 9
Carefully remove cupcakes from tin and leave to cool on wire rack

Step 10
Sift icing sugar and cocoa into a bowl. Pour in coffee and mix slightly

Step 11
Beat in butter until smooth and creamy. Spoon into piping bag

Step 12
Cut a nozzle 1 cm wide and pipe buttercream on each cupcake

Storage
Can be stored for up to three days in an air tight container

THE SCIENCY BIT

Ewww! What's that smell?

Coprolites are rocks that are made from poo that has been fossilised. The name is derived from Greek words *kopros*, meaning 'dung' and *lithos*, meaning 'stone'. Unlike fresh poo, coprolites do not smell.

Coprolites can range in size from a few millimetres to over 60 centimetres.

Did you know?
People who study coprolites are called Palaeoscatologists.

Mary Anning

Famous for collecting and studying Ichthyosaur (a prehistoric marine reptile) fossils from the coastal cliffs of Lyme Regis in Southwest England, Mary Anning discovered coprolites in the 1820's. Prior to this they were known as 'fossil fir cones' and 'bezoar stones' but no-one knew where they came from or how they were formed. It was Mary who began to notice that the mystery rocks were often found in the abdominal region of the ichthyosaur skeletons. When she broke some of them open she discovered fossilised fish bones, fish scales and bones of smaller ichthyosaurs. After sharing her observations with a geologist called William Buckland he proposed that 'bezoars' were actually fossilised poo and named them coprolites.

Ichthyosaur

What can we learn from fossilised poo?

Studying coprolites is really important as it can provide information on the diet of prehistoric animals. For example it is possible to determine if an animal was a herbivore or carnivore.

Belemnite

William Buckland recognised that the shape of the deposit was important to. He noticed that spiral markings on ichthyosaur coprolites indicated that the animals might have had spiral ridges in their intestines, similar to modern day sharks. He also noticed that some coprolites were stained black from the ink of swallowed belemnites.

Coprolite mining

In 1842 Reverend John Henslow realised the potential of coprolites as a use for fertiliser. He had discovered that by treating the fossils with sulphuric acid, phosphate could be released.

He patented his idea and set about mining on an industrial scale. Mining declined in the 1880s after the process for manufacturing artificial manure became easy and cheaper.

There is a street in Ipswich (UK) named Coprolite Street near the location of where coprolites were refined.

COPROLITE STREET

World record collection

In 2017 the Guinness Book of World Records declared George Frandsen the holder of the largest collection of coprolite fossils. It consists of 1277 different samples and is housed in the South Florida Museum in Bradenton, USA.

FRANKLIN'S DNA PASTA BAKE

Jake the dino top tips

You will need
- large casserole dish
- casserole lid or tinfoil
- oil for greasing
- knife
- large pan
- oven and grill

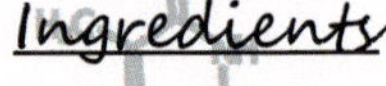

1 large onion
150 g chorizo
250 g asparagus
4 cloves garlic
1 tbsp olive oil
250 g fusilli pasta
1 kg passata (crushed tomatoes)
1 tbsp mixed herbs
Pinch of salt and pepper
300 ml pint of water
300 ml pint milk
200 g grated cheese

STEP 1

Pre-heat oven to 180 °C

STEP 2

Lightly grease a large casserole dish

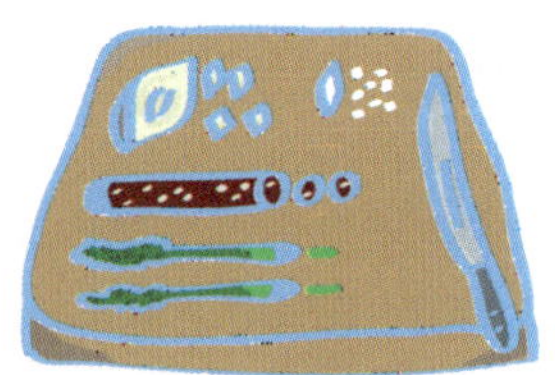

STEP 3

Dice the onion and chorizo, chop asparagus and crush the garlic

STEP 4

Heat oil in a large pan. Lower heat and add onion. Cook until soft

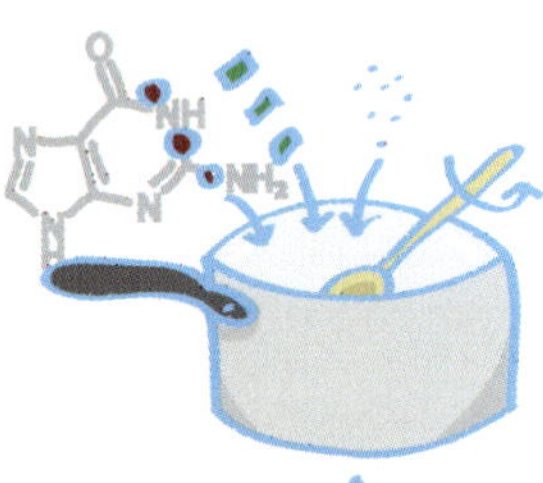

STEP 5

Add chorizo, garlic and asparagus. Cook for 10 minutes whilst stirring occasionally

STEP 6

Turn off the heat and stir in pasta, pasatta, herbs, salt, pepper, water and milk

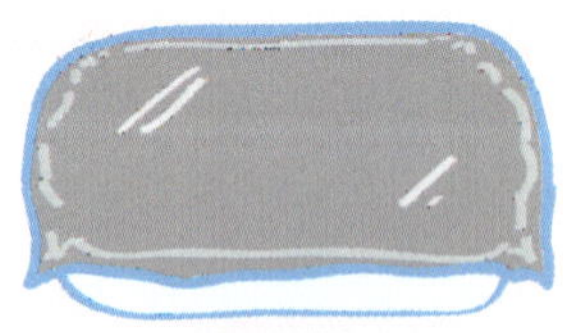

STEP 7

Pour into greased casserole dish and cover with lid or foil

Bake for 60 minutes. Clean up, set the table or read the sciency bit

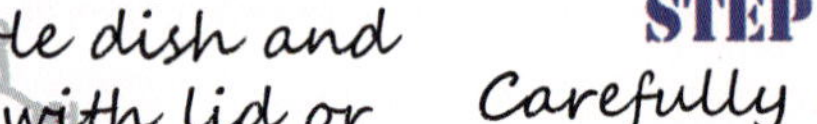

STEP 9

Carefully remove the lid. Use oven gloves to protect hands from steam

STEP 10

Sprinkle grated cheese over the pasta bake

STEP 11

Place the bake under a grill until cheese melts

Serve! Goes well with side salad

Steps 2 - 7 can be prepared 24 hours in advance. Keep refrigerated until ready to cook

THE SCIENCY BIT - THE CODE FOR LIFE

DNA is known as the building blocks for life as it contains all the code to create a living organism. The letters are an acronym for **D**eoxyribo**N**ucleic **A**cid. It was first observed in 1869 by a German biochemist, Frederich Miescher. It wasn't until the 1950's that the structure and its importance to life was discovered.

WHAT IS DNA?

CELLS have a number of structures that help them function. One of these is the **NUCLEUS**

Our bodies are made up of trillions of cells. Each cell has a special function that helps the body work. In the nucleus of each cell is a set of chromosomes. These chromosomes are made up of tightly wound up DNA.

DNA is a long thin molecule. It is made of three main parts; nucleotides, phosphate and deoxyribose. There are four different types of nucleotides; Adenine, Thymine, Cytosine and Guanine. Nucleotides are sometimes referred to as bases and come in pairs. In DNA Adenine is always paired with Thymine and Cytosine is always paired with Guanine.

Adenine Thymine Cytosine Guanine

Holding the nucleotides together is a backbone of phosphate and deoxyribose.

CHROMOSOMES are organised into pairs. In humans, 23 are inherited from your mother and 23 from your father

GLOSSARY
Molecule - A group of two or more atoms held together by chemical bonds e.g. H_2O

PHOSPHATE AND DEOXYRIBOSE BACKBONE

NUCLEOTIDES (BASES)

THE DNA CODE

The code that gives the instructions to a cell on how to perform its function is held within the order of the nucleotides. Every three letters are grouped into a codon. This allows for billions of code combinations. A group of codons is called a gene.

CODON GENE

T G C C T G A C G A T T G C T A A G C A T A C C G A T C G T T

Genes are responsible for determining physical characteristics such as eye colour. Humans have approximately 20,000 genes. One copy of all your chromosomes is called a genome.

DID YOU KNOW?
The DNA code in every human is unique to them except in the cases of identical siblings. The first time DNA was used to solve a crime was in 1988.

ROSALIND FRANKLIN

Rosalind Franklin was born in London in 1920. After studying chemistry at Cambridge University and in Paris, she specialised in x-ray crystallography. This technique uses x-ray beams to determine structures at the atomic and molecular scale.

Throughout her career she contributed to the understanding of structures of viruses, coal and graphite. Her work helped with the understanding of which coal provided better fuel. This knowledge was used throughout World War II. Her most important discovery contributed to the discovery of the structure of DNA.

ROSALIND FRANKLIN

PHOTO 51 is a x-ray diffraction image of crystallised DNA. The photo became a key data source for determining the structure of DNA.

In 2020 the European and Russian space agencies plan to launch a mission to the planet Mars. The solar powered rover is named after Franklin and will complete a seven month mission in search for the existence of past Martian life.

Primordial Noodle Soup

What came first, the chicken or the egg? A fun question that makes you think about how life got started here on Earth. 'Primordial soup' is the name given to one of the theories and makes the perfect name for this recipe. We may not have figured out the answer yet but tuck into this tasty, heart-warming soup to learn about what we know so far.

Jake the dino top tips

You will need

- knife
- chopping board
- slotted spoon
- ladle
- 2 pans

Ingredients

- 2 chicken breasts
- salt and pepper
- 1 tbsp vegetable oil
- 190 g rice noodles
- 3 cabbage leaves
- 8 baby corn
- 2 spring onion
- 2 eggs
- 1 clove of garlic (chopped)
- 1 tbsp ginger
- 2 tbsp lemon juice
- 2 tbsp honey
- 1 chilli (chopped)
- 800 ml chicken stock

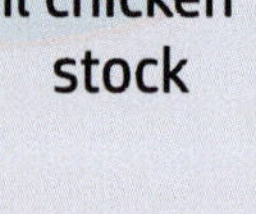

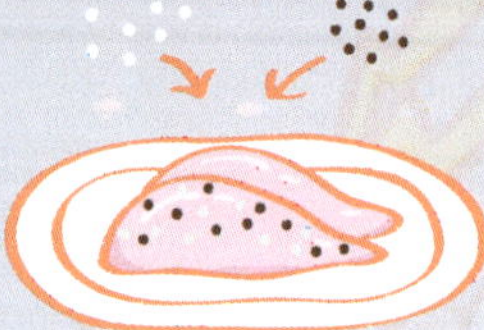

Step 1
Season chicken with salt and pepper

Step 2
Heat oil in a pan. Cook chicken on high heat for one minute on each side

Step 3
Turn heat down and cook chicken for 15 minutes until cooked through. Set to one side

Step 4
Boil water and cook noodles

Step 5
Drain and distribute amongst four bowls

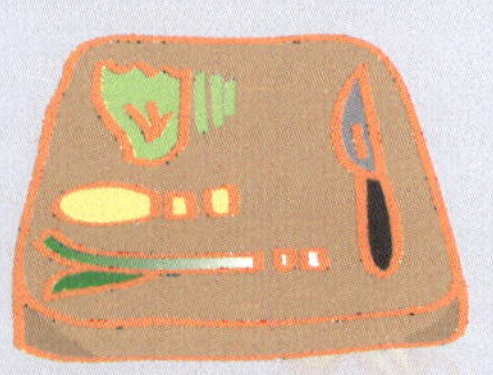

Step 6
Cut vegetables into bite size chunks

Step 7
Place vegetables on noodles

Step 8
Boil water, cook eggs for 7 mins

Step 9
Use slotted spoon to take eggs out of water. Run under cold water for 20 seconds

Step 10
Peel, cut in half and put on noodles. Slice chicken place on noodles

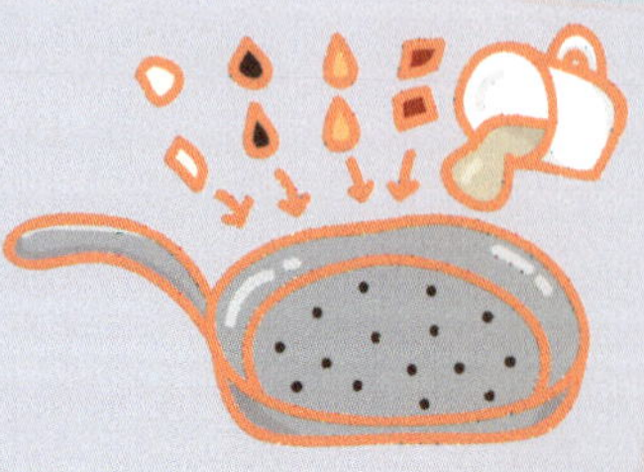

Step 11
In pan with chicken juice lightly fry garlic, ginger, lemon juice, honey, chilli. Add stock

Step 12
Bring stock to boil before ladelling over noodles. Serve

Good to know

It is easy to turn this into a vegetarian meal. Either omit the chicken or swap for tofu.

--

Steps 1 - 10 can be prepared up to 24 hours in advance. Just keep refrigerated until ready to eat.

The Sciency Bit - What came first, the chicken or the egg?

The natural process of how life started is scientifically known as abiogenesis. Scientists who study abiogenesis try to work out how non-living matter such as carbon and oxygen were used to create living, organic matter. The generation of the complex life we recognise today is thought to have happened through a series of chemical reactions and molecular evolution over millions of years. Scientists follow two different methods to figure out how this happened. These are called the top-down approach and the bottom-up approach. The top-down method starts from what we know about life today and works backwards to the origin. The bottom-up approach starts from the beginning and tries to work out what was needed for life to start. So far it is only possible to take the process as far back as single-cell organisms. Scientists are yet to work out how simple life was created.

An elephant is considered 'complex life' because it is made up of trillions of cells each working together to keep an animal alive.

Bottom-up

Top-down

A single-cell organism is considered 'simple life' because it is made up of one cell that uses basic functions to stay alive.

The Primordial Soup theory

The primordial theory is part of the bottom-up approach. It was first proposed by Alexander Oparin in 1924 and John Burdon Sanderson Haldane in 1929. Their theories described a set of conditions in the primitive atmosphere on Earth that led to basic elements such as carbon and hydrogen being turned into the first organic compounds, known as monomers. These simple compounds accumulated in a 'soup' and by further transformation formed complex organic compounds, known as polymers. DNA (Deoxyribonucleic Acid) is an example of a polymer which is made of monomers called amino acids. DNA is a vital component in the cells of complex life that exists today.

The Miller-Urey experiment

Stanley Miller and Harold Urey designed a chemical experiment to test Oparin's and Haldane's hypothesis for the origin of life. It was conducted in 1952 and is considered to be the classic experiment investigating abiogenesis.

Different parts of the experiment were designed to simulate the environment of a primitive Earth.

① Water was heated to produce vapour. A vacuum pump forced the vapour to circulate around the apparatus

② The water vapour mixed with gases

③ Continuous electrical sparks provide energy

④ Cold water is used to cool the vapour to condense it back into a liquid

⑤ The liquid is collected in a trap and sampled with a probe

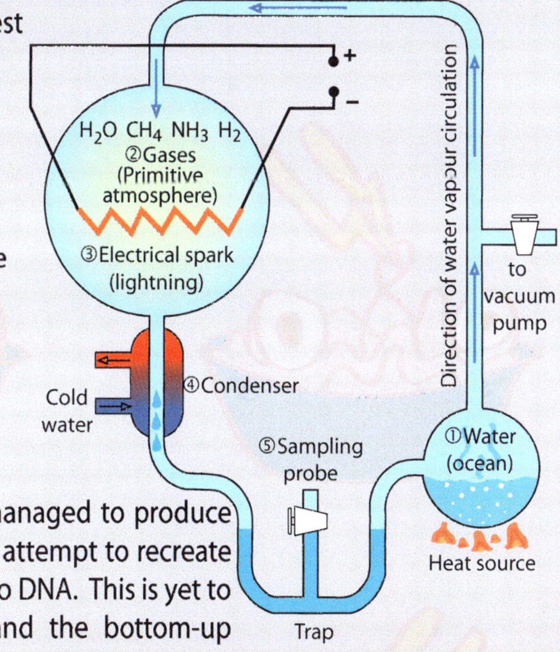

The results of the experiment reported that Miller and Urey had managed to produce amino acid monomers. This experiment inspired other scientists to attempt to recreate the conditions on primitive earth in order to turn the amino acids into DNA. This is yet to be discovered and therefore the link between the top-down and the bottom-up approach is yet to be made.

Dragonfly, NASA

Future Research

In June 2019 NASA selected the Dragonfly mission for launch in 2026. Its mission is to send a mobile robotic rotocraft to Titan, the largest moon of Saturn. The atmosphere of Titan is thought to be similar to that of early Earth.

The aim of the study will be to conduct chemical analysis to support the origin of life experiments here on Earth. It will also see if it can detect complex monomers and therefore the possibility of life forming on a different planet to our own.

TURING'S BANANA SPLIT BOMBE GLACÉE

Jake the dino top tips

You will need

- 2 litre pudding basin
- cling film
- knife
- chopping board
- piping bag
- serving plate

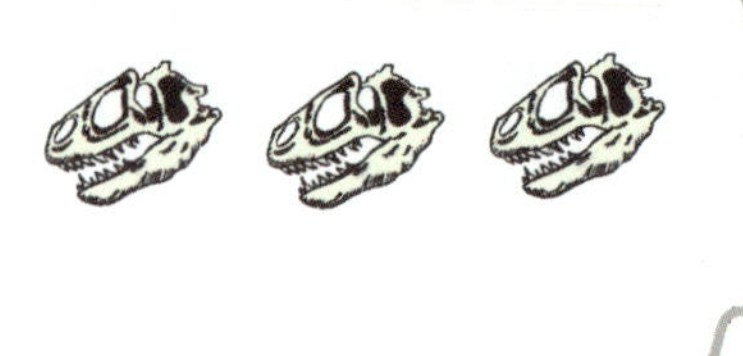

Ingredients: you will need to use the cypher below to translate the list

A	B	C	D	E	F	G	H	I	J	K	L	M	N	O	P	Q	R	S	T	U	V	W	X	Y	Z
J	S	B	W	L	D	U	X	M	P	N	A	R	G	K	Z	C	O	V	H	Y	I	T	Q	F	E

500 ml BWMLDCZMMU VQZQMZLI __________ ________

7 CLKLKLB _______

500 ml SLKVEEL VQZQMZLI _______ ________

500 ml QTRQRELWZ VQZQMZLI _________ ________

150 ml FRGCEZ QMZLI ______ _____

100 g VQVKN BGNLM _____ _____

1 tbsp DLWZM _____

100 g QTRQRELWZ CGWWRKB _________ _______

150 g QTRQRELWZ QTVJB _________ _____

200 g NELQZ QTZMMVZB _____ ________

50 g QTRJJZF KGWB _______ ____

1 can BXGVMWU QMZLI _______ _____

10 g BJMVKOEZB _________

Step 1

Line a pudding basin with cling film

Step 2

Get the strawberry ice cream out and let it soften

Step 3

Squash the ice cream into the pudding basin until a 1/4 full

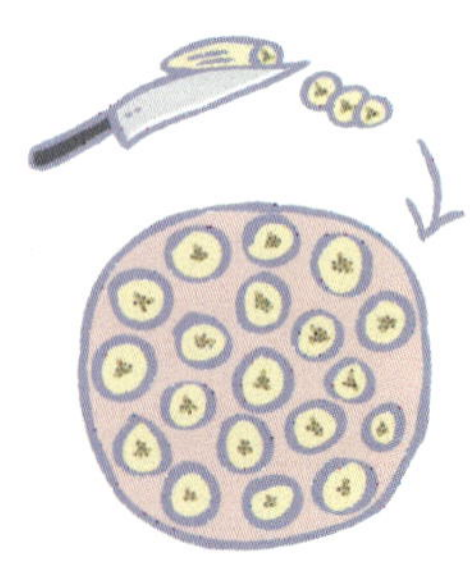

Step 4

Spread sliced banana on top of ice cream to form a layer

TOP SECRET

Step 5
Repeat steps 2-4 with vanilla and chocolate icecream

2+ hrs

Step 6
Put back in the freezer for at least two hours

Step 7
Sift icing sugar and water to form a thick paste. Spoon into piping bag. Write a coded message using chocolate buttons. Leave to dry

Step 8
Just before serving heat up double cream in a pan. When small bubbles form take off heat and stir in chocolate chips

Step 9
Turn pudding bowl upside down on serving plate. Lift bowl and plastic film off

Step 10
Pour the cooled chocolate sauce over the bombe. Decorate with cherries, nuts, sprinkles and squirty cream

Step 11
Spell secret message with chocolate buttons you decorated earlier

Step 12
Serve! Don't forget to give the cypher to your friend, so they can translate the secret message

THE SCIENCY BIT - Breaking the Enigma Code

Codes have been used for centuries to pass secrets between people. The message can only be written and understood by those who have the cypher. In World War II the Germans used an Enigma machine to code messages. It was up to those that lived and worked at Bletchley Park to work out how to break it.

Bletchley Park

Bletchley Park was the home of the codebreakers throughout World War II. It was bought in 1938 by the head of the Secret Intelligence Service (now MI6) for use by the Government Code and Cypher School. When war broke out in 1939 the work done by codebreakers focused on trying to decypher the Enigma code.

What was Enigma?

Enigma was a machine invented by the German engineer Arthur Scherbius and created to encrypt messages. It was used by the German military throughout World War II to send coded messages. The machine had a possible 15,000,000,000,000,000,00 (15 billion billion) combinations making it seemingly impossible to decode.

The Bombe Machine

The bombe was an electromechanical device designed by Alan Turing and Gordon Welchman at Bletchley Park. The design meant that it could perform calculations faster than any human. It was able to recover the key settings the Germans used when writing codes on their Enigma machines thus allowing the codebreakers to decypher messages received via radio listening stations.

Throughout the war different versions of the bombe machine were built to keep up with different variations of enigma machines built by the Germans. They were housed at various sites across the UK in case one site was bombed. Each machine was approximately 2 meters high, 2 meters wide, ½ meter deep and weighed about a ton. The Wrens (Women's Royal Naval Service) played a vital role in the operation with some 700 women operating over two hundred bombes.

Alan Turing

Alan Turing was a British mathematician who worked at Bletchley Park during World War II. After the war he continued his work on computer science, mathematics and artificial intelligence. He created the first detailed design of a stored-computer programme and developed an experiment to define the standard for a machine's intelligence. His work contributed to the design of computers that we use today.

Alan Turing

In 1954 Turing committed suicide. Two years previous to this he was prosecuted for homosexual acts, as 'gross indecency' was considered illegal at that time. In 2009, the government apologised for Turing's prosecution as a homosexual. In 2014, The Queen officially pardoned Turing which in turn led to an inquiry into the exoneration of every man that was convicted of similar historical indecency offences. The 'Alan Turing Law' came into effect in 2016 and serves to retroactively pardon men who were cautioned or convicted under historical legislation that outlawed homosexual acts.

After the war

The work done at Bletchley Park remained top secret for many years after the war. It is only within the last 20 years that its importance in shortening the war has been recognised. The site was at risk of demolition until a Trust was formed to protect it. After raising £8 million, a restoration project was completed in 2014 with a number of exhibitions outlining the site's history and legacy.

Why not visit?

Bletchley Park is located 10 minutes south of Milton Keynes, England. It is open all year round and has both indoor and outdoor activities. There's a bonus - tickets are valid for an entire year!

EARTH

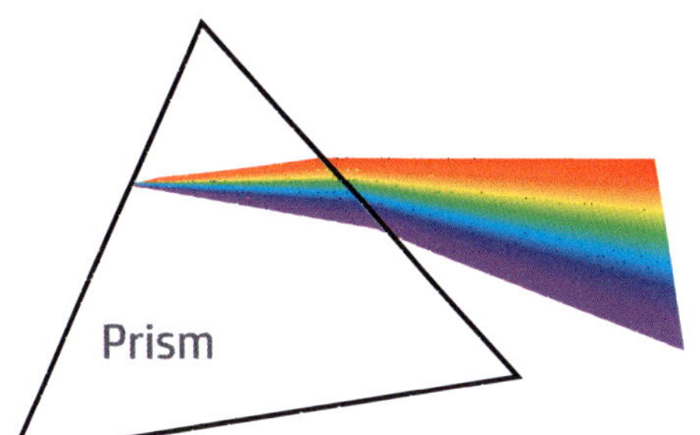

Rainbow Rice 28

This recipe uses vegetables from all the colours of the rainbow to teach you about a naturally occurring optical illusion. You will learn about the different properties of light waves and what unique weather events need to occur in order to observe a rainbow. This recipe can be cooked on a BBQ or in an oven.

Meitner's Fission Cheesecake 30

Popping candy and the sweet and sour taste of lemon cheesecake makes a perfect combination to explain about nuclear fission. You will learn about the woman who discovered how to split the atom in order to create vast amounts of energy.

Uranium isotope 325 nucleus

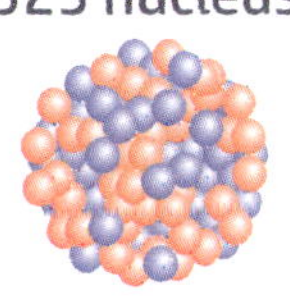

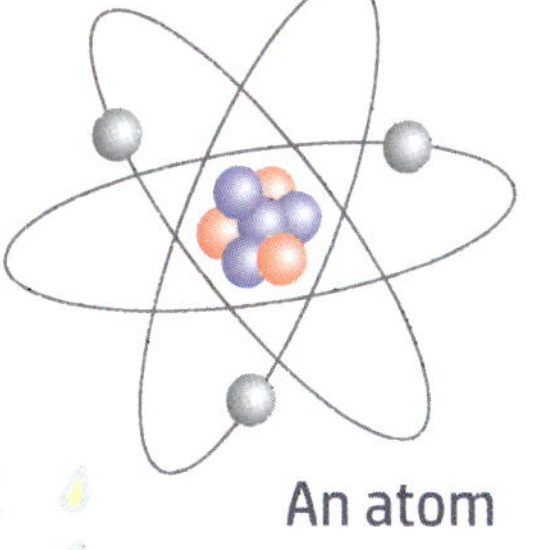

An atom

Journey to the Centre of the Pizza 32

Fresh home-made pizza tastes the best! This recipe uses different toppings to teach you what the different layers of the Earth are thousands of kilometers below your feet.

Inge Lehmann

Rainbow Rice with BBQ chicken

Serves 4

Rainbows aren't objects but rather optical illusions caused by sunlight and rain. This recipe uses colourful vegetables baked with rice and chicken to make a yummy meal that helps you learn about how they form.

Rice

15 g butter
1 red pepper
1 orange pepper
2 red onions
1 clove of garlic
1 tin of sweetcorn
200 g frozen peas
200 g rice
650 ml of chicken stock
50 ml tomato sauce

Chicken

30 g fajita BBQ spice mix
2 tbsp honey
1 tbsp lime juice
2 tbsp olive oil
salt and pepper
8 chicken thighs, wings or breasts

Coleslaw

1 small cabbage
5 carrots (peeled)
100 g mayonnaise
50 g sultanas
salt and pepper

Jake the dino top tips

You will need
- Casserole dish
- Tin foil
- Roasting tin
- Knife & chopping board

Good to know

Step 7 can be prepared 24 hours in advance. Cover bowl in cling film and store in fridge

Step 1
Pre-heat oven to 160 °C and grease the casserole dish with butter

Step 2
Dice the peppers, onions and garlic

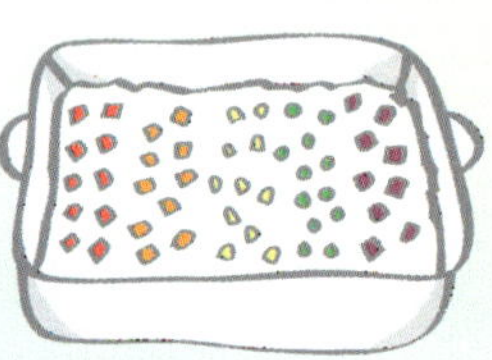

Step 3
Add rice, chopped veg, sweetcorn and peas to casserole dish

Step 4
Make stock in a jug and stir in tomato sauce

Step 5
Pour stock over rice and stir

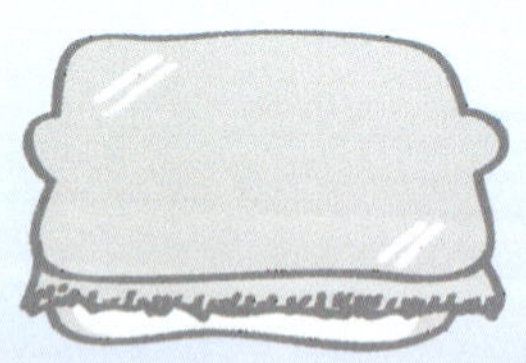

Step 6
Wrap tin foil over the casserole dish making sure that it is sealed tight around the edges

Step 7
Mix all the chicken ingredients in a bowl before adding the chicken

Step 8
Place chicken in the roasting tin

Step 9
Cook the rice and chicken for 50 minutes

Step 10
Grate the cabbage and carrots. Mix in the rest of the coleslaw ingredients

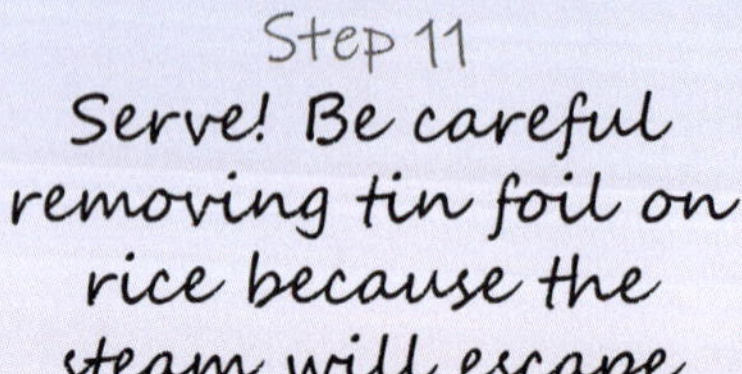

Step 11
Serve! Be careful removing tin foil on rice because the steam will escape

Good to know

This recipe can be cooked on a BBQ. Prepare the coleslaw in advance and use a metal casserole dish.

The Sciency Bit! Red and orange and pink and green...

Rainbows are a weather phenomenon that can be seen in the sky. To form they need both rainfall and sunlight to occur at the same time. It is important to understand some fundamental properties of light to understand how a rainbow forms.

Properties of light

Scientists have discovered that light can either behave as a particle, a physical object called a Photon, or as a wave in the Electromagnetic Spectrum. This is because observations they make about the behaviour of light, in nature and through experiments, can be explained either as a wave or a particle. Physicists call this concept 'wave-particle duality'. When looking at a rainbow we need to think in terms of light being a wave.

Newton's prism experiments

In 1704 Isaac Newton published a book called 'Opticks'. In it he showed that with the use of a prism he was able to disperse the white light and prove that it is made up of all the colours we can see.

A prism is a transparent optical element with flat, polished surfaces

White light

Dispersion when white light is split into its component parts

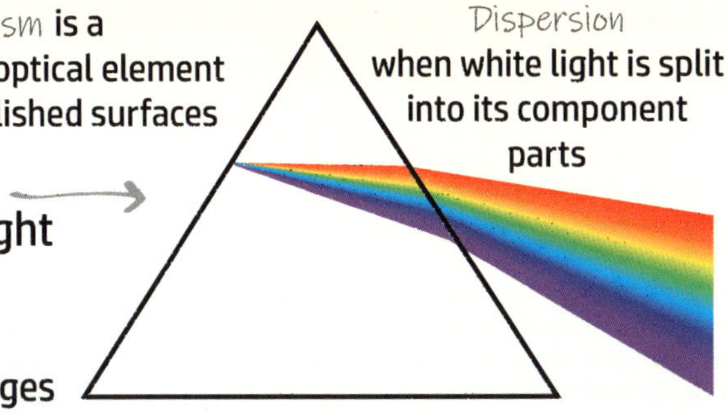

Huygens-Fresnel principle

When a light wave passes from one medium to another it changes speed and gets bent slightly. The prism and the air surrounding it have different densities so the light gets bent once when it enters the prism and a second time when the light exits the prism.

Refraction is the bending of light as it passes from one substance to another

Snell's Law

How much a light wave gets bent when it passes from one density to another is dependent on two things. The difference between the densities of the two mediums the light passes through, called the *refractive index,* and the angle at which the wave enters the prism.

Red light has a longer wavelength than violet light. When the white light enters the prism and gets refracted the red end of the colour spectrum gets bent slightly less than the violet end. This causes the dispersion that Isaac Newton observed with his prisms.

Red light has a wavelength of between 700-635 nm

Violet light has a wavelength of between 450-400 nm

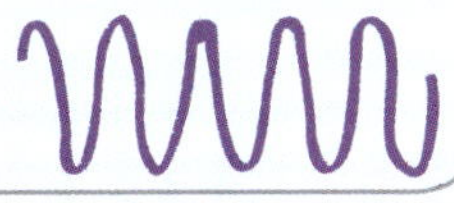

How a rainbow forms

A rainbow in the sky is formed because raindrops act like prisms. Sunlight enters the raindrop, gets refracted and dispersed. The spectrum of colours is reflected off the back surface of the raindrop and as it exits the raindrop gets refracted again. Many rainbows will be produced but you will only observe one that is unique to your location. Due to dispersion you will see red light from raindrops higher in the sky moving through the spectrum to raindrops lower in the sky.

Did you know? The sun will always be behind you when you see a rainbow form

Sunlight

Reflection occurs when a light ray hits a surface and bounces off

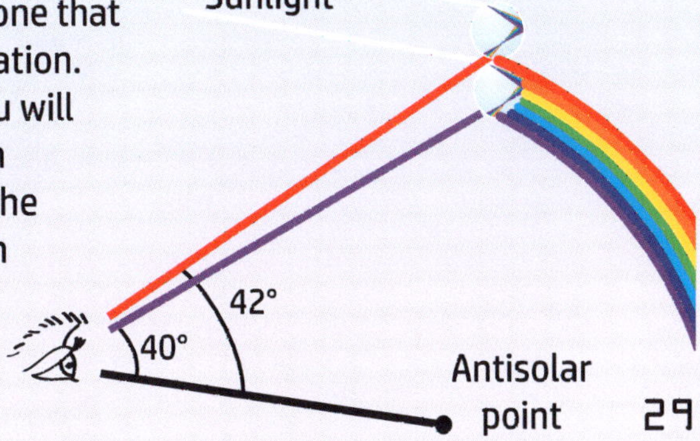

Rain drop

Sunlight

42°

40°

Antisolar point

Meitner's Fission Cheesecake

Ingredients

Base
200 g chocolate biscuits
100 g butter

Cheesecake
500 g cream cheese
120 g caster sugar
zest of 2 lemons
2 eggs
2 egg whites

Lemon curd
2 egg yolks
Juice of 2 lemons
120 g caster sugar
40 g butter

Decoration
100 g chocolate coated popping candy

This mouth-tingling cheesecake is flavoured with lemon and decorated with popping candy. It introduces the process of nuclear fission, who discovered the process and the uses for it.

Jake the dino top tips

You will need

- Bag
- 20 cm springform cake tin

Step 1
Pre-heat oven to 160° C

Step 2
Place biscuits in bag. Crush into crumbs using a rolling pin

Step 3
Melt butter in a pan. Stir in biscuit crumbs. Press mixture into bottom of cake tin

Step 4
Separate two eggs into two bowls. Set the yolks to one side

Step 5
Add the remaining eggs, lemon zest, caster sugar and cream cheese to egg whites. Whisk until well combined

Step 6
Pour mixture into cake tin and smooth flat. Bake in oven for 30 minutes

Step 7
Turn off oven, open door slightly and leave to cool

Step 8
Add lemon juice, caster sugar and butter to bowl with egg yolks

Step 9
Put bowl over a pan of simmering water. Keep stirring until thickened. Leave to cool

Step 10
Spread curd mixture over cheesecake. Leave to set in fridge for 2 hours

Step 11
Place tin on a mug. Slide cake tin side down. Carefully slide cheesecake off the base onto serving plate

Step 12
Use popping candy to decorate the cheese cake with nuclear hazard symbol

The Sciency Bit - Splitting the Atom

AN ATOM

NUCLEUS

ELECTRON

NEUTRON

PROTON

Atoms are what make up all the things you can see around you. They are very small and cannot be seen by the naked eye. Every atom is comprised of a nucleus that contains protons and neutrons. Orbiting the nucleus are electrons. The number of protons and neutrons in each atom defines the element it will make. Fission is a process where the nucleus is split apart. When this happens naturally it is called radioactive decay.

Man-made Nuclear Fusion

In the 1930's a small group of scientists designed a way of creating man-made nuclear fission. They accomplished this by firing a neutron at the nucleus of an Uranium atom. The result led to the Uranium atom splitting into two smaller nuclei accompanied by an enormous release of energy.

What is an isotope?

The total number of protons and neutrons in an atom defines the mass number. Isotopes are the atoms of an element with different numbers of neutrons. They have the same proton number, but different mass numbers.

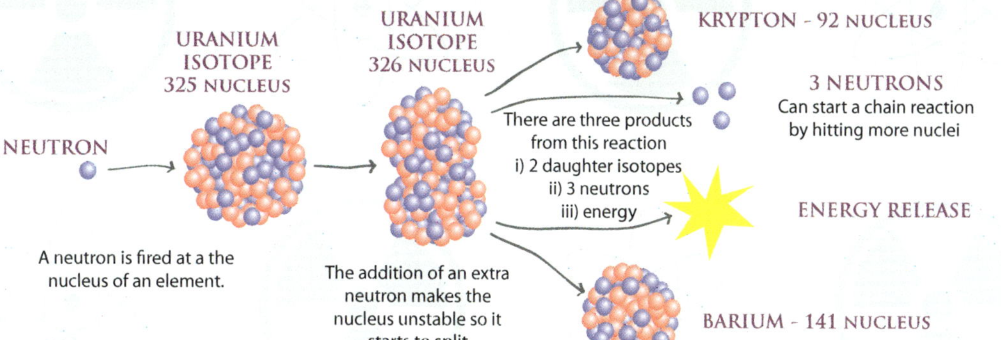

Nuclear Energy

The huge amounts of energy that nuclear fission generates produces huge amounts of heat. Nuclear power stations utilise this heat to turn steam turbines in order to produce electricity. Many countries around the world have built nuclear power stations in order to produce energy for its citizens.

Harnessing nuclear energy is cause for scientific, social and political debate. Unlike burning fossil fuels, nuclear power does not release CO_2 into the atmosphere. However the process does produce radioactive waste which is hazardous to humans and other living organisms. It can take millions of years for the waste to decay so safe places to store it need to be found. Choosing them can be controversial, especially to locals who may live near by.

There are also issues surrounding the safety of nuclear power stations. High profile accidents at Three Mile Island (1979), Chernobyl (1986) and Fukushima (2011) have led to many square kilometers of land being contaminated. Land where people once lived and farmed may never be used again.

Lise Meitner

Lise Meitner, born in 1878, was an Austrian-Swedish physicist who worked on radioactivity and nuclear physics. She led the team that was first to discover nuclear fission.

She was the first women to become a full professor of physics in Germany but ultimately lost this position in the 1930's with the introduction of the anti-Jewish Nuremberg Laws of Nazi Germany. She fled to Sweden and eventually became a Swedish citizen.

In 1944 her long-time collaborator, Otto Hahn, was awarded the Nobel Prize in Chemistry for the discovery of nuclear fission. In the 1990's, the Nobel committee's proceedings were made public. A paper published in the journal Physics Today stated, "Meitner's exclusion from the chemistry award may well be summarized as a mixture of disciplinary bias, political obtuseness, ignorance, and haste." In 1997 she had the chemical element 109, Meitnerium, named after her.

"Science makes people reach selflessly for truth and objectivity; it teaches people to accept reality, with wonder and admiration, not to mention the deep awe and joy that the natural order of things brings to the true scientist."
Lise Meitner

Q- What did the nuclear physicist have for lunch?

A - Fission chips!

Journey to the Centre of the Pizza

Pineapple on a pizza? Yummy for some, controversial for others and can be easily changed for other toppings just so long as you follow the recipe whilst decorating the pizza. Read the 'sciency bit' to learn all about the different layers of the Earth.

Jake the dino top tips

You will need
- Rolling pin
- Baking trays

Pizza dough

550 g strong bread flour
7 g yeast
1 ½ tbsp caster sugar
¼ tsp salt
3 tbsp olive oil
320 ml warm water

Sauce

500 g passata
1 tbsp dried basil
¼ tsp salt
1 tsp pepper
1 tbsp chopped garlic

Topping

300 g grated cheese
24 slices of pepperoni
1 red pepper (diced)
150 g pineapple chunks

Makes four 9" pizzas

Step 1
Sift flour, salt and sugar into a bowl. Add yeast, olive oil and warm water

Step 2
Mix into a dough and then knead for 5 minutes on a floured surface

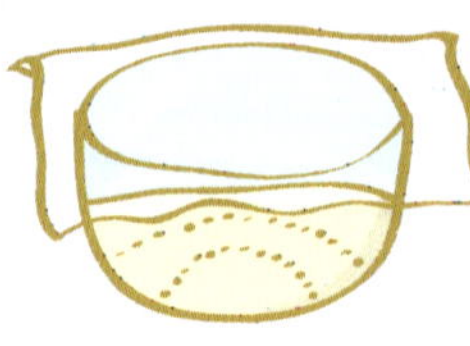

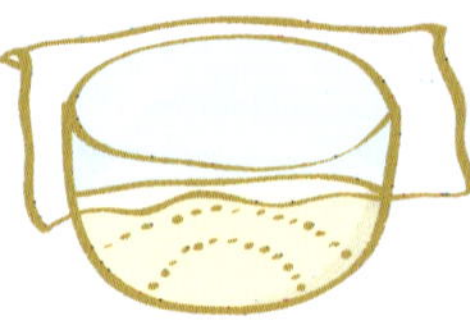

Step 3
Put dough back into bowl and cover with cling film. Leave in a warm place for 1 hour

Step 4
Pre-heat oven to 180° C

Step 5
Punch out the air and split the dough into 4 pieces

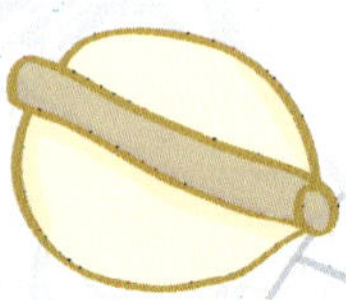

Step 6
On a floured surface roll a piece of dough out to 9" diameter and place on baking tray

Step 7
Mix together passata, basil, salt, pepper and garlic

Step 8
Spread tomato sauce on pizza followed by grated cheese

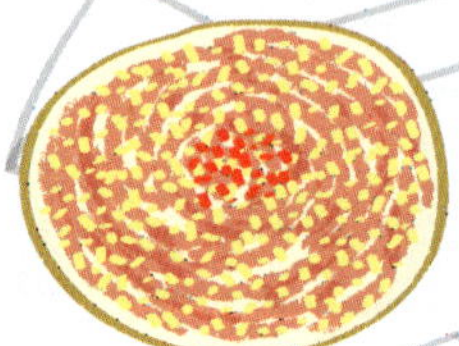

Step 9
Place peppers in the centre of the pizza

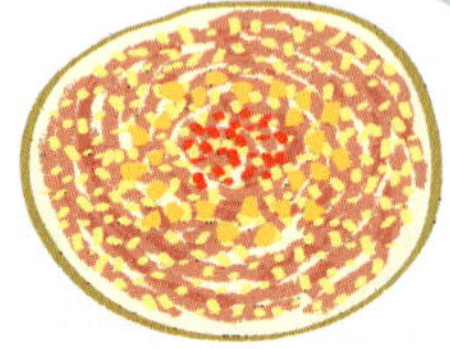

Step 10
Sprinkle pineapple around the peppers

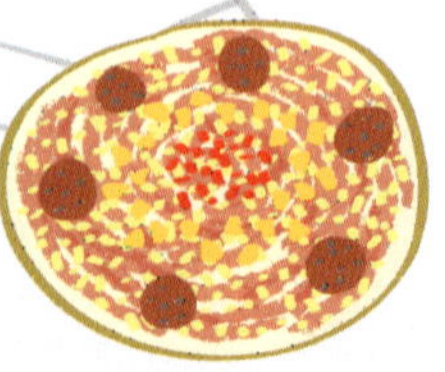

Step 11
Place six pieces of pepperoni around the pineapple

Step 12
Repeat steps 6 - 11 for remaining 3 pieces of dough. Bake for 25 minutes. Carefully remove from oven. Cut into slices between pepperoni

THE SCIENCY BIT "You won't find anything edible in there"

Jules Verne, Journey to the Centre of the Earth

The internal structure of the Earth defines how life on Earth has evolved over geological time. It can be split into four main layers; the crust, mantle, outer core and inner core. The Earth has a radius of 6360 km.

CRUST

Volcanoes help form new rock

Subduction zones help recycle old rock by melting in mantle

5-70 km

MANTLE

2830 km

OUTER CORE

2200 km

INNER CORE

1260 km

Do you know? It would take 38 minutes to fall through the Earth

CRUST

The crust is the hard rocky outer layer of the Earth. The crust is broken into parts called plates that move around. The Earth is the only planet in our Solar System to have active plate tectonics.

There are two types of crust; continental crust, that carries land and oceanic crust, that carries water.

MANTLE

The mantle is the thickest layer. Heat rising and falling inside the mantle creates convection currents generated by radioactive decay in the core.

The convection currents help drive the movement of the plates above. Where plates meet is called a 'plate boundary'. Earthquakes and volcanoes are most likely to occur on or near these boundaries.

OUTER CORE

The outer core is made of molten iron and nickel. Scientific models suggest that eddy currents in the metal fluid, driven by heat escaping the core, could influence the Earth's magnetic field. This natural process is called a geodynamo.

INNER CORE

Solid ball of iron and nickel.
It was discovered in 1936 by Inge Lehmann.
Temperatures can reach 5400 °C.

Inge Lehmann

Inge Lehmann was a Danish seismologist and geophysicist. She spent her career studying the structure of the Earth, a field of science called geodetics.

Lehmann would use sound waves created by earthquakes to discover the structure of the Earth. As well as the inner core she also discovered another seismic discontinuity. Named after her, the Lehmann discontinuity can only be found under continental crust. which lies at depths between 190 km and 250 km.

To mark the 100th year of women's suffrage in Denmark she had a beetle named after her called *Globicornis ingelehmannae.*

"Science, my boy, is made up of mistakes, but they are mistakes which it is useful to make, because they lead little by little to the truth"
Jules Verne,
Journey to the Centre of the Earth

Do you know? The opposite point on the Earth to where you are now is called the antipode.

INDEX - Ingredients

INDEX - Science

Want to learn more? Go to www.scirecipes.co.uk

Tweet us @SciRecipes

Send us a message or share your pictures on our SciRecipes pages

Got a question? E-mail us at enquire@scirecipes.co.uk

Printed in Great Britain
by Amazon

67424749R00022